FRIENDSHIP

This book belongs to

_____

In Denmark, we use a special
word—hygge—to describe a
feeling of coziness, security,
and togetherness.

This book is filled with questions to help capture the essence of your friends on paper, so that you can revisit their thoughts whenever you'd like. Some of the questions may seem simple, but in reality we often don't get around to knowing basic things about each other. These pages offer an opportunity to take a moment to learn something about your friends—and to read how they feel about you and your friendship.

How did you come to receive this book? Maybe it was given to you on an important occasion, where the book was passed around for all of your friends to fill in. Perhaps you plan to ask your friends to write in it one by one, over a period of time. Either way, you'll have some great conversations and will end up with a record of how much you and your friends mean to each other.

Friends are crucial at various stages and moments in life. Turn to this book whenever you need a laugh or some support. Unlike a post on social media—which can be seen and commented upon by anyone—these messages were written just for you.

In Denmark, where we are from, we use a special word—hygge (pronounced hoo-ga)—to describe a feeling of coziness, security, and togetherness. Hygge is how you feel with your closest friends; that sense you can just relax and be yourself. We hope that this book gives you that feeling every time you open it!

— *Lisa and Maise*

DATE _____

My friend, please answer these questions about yourself . . .

Your name is _____

Your birthday is _____ and currently you are _____ years old

If you had to describe yourself in three words, they would be _____
_____

When you were little, you wanted to be a _____

You still dream about becoming a _____

If you won the lottery, you would spend it on _____

The best book you've read so far is _____

One of your favorite movies is _____

Your favorite color is _____

Your favorite animal is _____

You love the scent of _____

You have a secret crush on _____

Your hero is _____

You are very good at _____

You want to be better at _____

Your one regret is _____

The three biggest changes in your life have been _____
_____
_____

Now, your thoughts about me . . .

If you had to describe me in three words, they would be

If I were an animal I would be a(n)

The famous person I most resemble is

If I won the lottery, I would probably spend it on

If I ruled the world, there would be

You know that I have a crush on

Two things that you appreciate most about me are

And finally, about us!

We became friends when

One of the funniest moments of our friendship was

If you and I were characters in a book, movie, or on TV, we would be

The song that reminds you of us is

The thing that we have the most in common is

Our biggest difference is

Your favorite thing about our friendship is

DATE

My friend, please answer these questions about yourself . . .

Your name is

Your birthday is _____ and currently you are _____ years old

If you had to describe yourself in three words, they would be

When you were little, you wanted to be a

You still dream about becoming a

If you won the lottery, you would spend it on

The best book you've read so far is

One of your favorite movies is

Your favorite color is

Your favorite animal is

You love the scent of

You have a secret crush on

Your hero is

You are very good at

You want to be better at

Your one regret is

The three biggest changes in your life have been

Now, your thoughts about me . . .

If you had to describe me in three words, they would be

If I were an animal I would be a(n)

The famous person I most resemble is

If I won the lottery, I would probably spend it on

If I ruled the world, there would be

You know that I have a crush on

Two things that you appreciate most about me are

And finally, about us!

We became friends when

One of the funniest moments of our friendship was

If you and I were characters in a book, movie, or on TV, we would be

The song that reminds you of us is

The thing that we have the most in common is

Our biggest difference is

Your favorite thing about our friendship is

DATE

My friend, please answer these questions about yourself . . .

Your name is

Your birthday is   and currently you are   years old

If you had to describe yourself in three words, they would be

When you were little, you wanted to be a

You still dream about becoming a

If you won the lottery, you would spend it on

The best book you've read so far is

One of your favorite movies is

Your favorite color is

Your favorite animal is

You love the scent of

You have a secret crush on

Your hero is

You are very good at

You want to be better at

Your one regret is

The three biggest changes in your life have been

Now, your thoughts about me . . .

If you had to describe me in three words, they would be _____

_____

If I were an animal I would be a(n) _____

The famous person I most resemble is _____

If I won the lottery, I would probably spend it on _____

If I ruled the world, there would be _____

You know that I have a crush on _____

Two things that you appreciate most about me are _____

_____

And finally, about us!

We became friends when _____

One of the funniest moments of our friendship was _____

_____

If you and I were characters in a book, movie, or on TV, we would be _____

_____

The song that reminds you of us is _____

The thing that we have the most in common is _____

Our biggest difference is _____

Your favorite thing about our friendship is _____

_____

DATE _____ _____

My friend, please answer these questions about yourself . . .

Your name is _____

Your birthday is _____ and currently you are _____ years old

If you had to describe yourself in three words, they would be _____

_____

When you were little, you wanted to be a _____

You still dream about becoming a _____

If you won the lottery, you would spend it on _____

The best book you've read so far is _____

One of your favorite movies is _____

Your favorite color is _____

Your favorite animal is _____

You love the scent of _____

You have a secret crush on _____

Your hero is _____

You are very good at _____

You want to be better at _____

Your one regret is _____

The three biggest changes in your life have been _____

_____

_____

Now, your thoughts about me . . .

If you had to describe me in three words, they would be

If I were an animal I would be a(n)

The famous person I most resemble is

If I won the lottery, I would probably spend it on

If I ruled the world, there would be

You know that I have a crush on

Two things that you appreciate most about me are

And finally, about us!

We became friends when

One of the funniest moments of our friendship was

If you and I were characters in a book, movie, or on TV, we would be

The song that reminds you of us is

The thing that we have the most in common is

Our biggest difference is

Your favorite thing about our friendship is

DATE

My friend, please answer these questions about yourself . . .

Your name is

Your birthday is   and currently you are   years old

If you had to describe yourself in three words, they would be

When you were little, you wanted to be a

You still dream about becoming a

If you won the lottery, you would spend it on

The best book you've read so far is

One of your favorite movies is

Your favorite color is

Your favorite animal is

You love the scent of

You have a secret crush on

Your hero is

You are very good at

You want to be better at

Your one regret is

The three biggest changes in your life have been

Now, your thoughts about me . . .

If you had to describe me in three words, they would be

If I were an animal I would be a(n)

The famous person I most resemble is

If I won the lottery, I would probably spend it on

If I ruled the world, there would be

You know that I have a crush on

Two things that you appreciate most about me are

And finally, about us!

We became friends when

One of the funniest moments of our friendship was

If you and I were characters in a book, movie, or on TV, we would be

The song that reminds you of us is

The thing that we have the most in common is

Our biggest difference is

Your favorite thing about our friendship is

Making New Friends

So, you've met someone that you feel you have a connection with. Someone you'd like to get to know better and develop a friendship with. Now what do you do?

It seems like everyone forgets how to make friends once they grow up. Somewhere along the way, it turns from something we do effortlessly into quite an intimidating prospect. It feels much more complicated, more challenging, and fraught with rejection. What if they don't feel the same connection you do? How will you fit into each other's lives? What if they don't get along with the friends you already have or vice versa?

Speaking of those friends who are already a part of your life, how did that happen in the first place? Maybe you just hung out in school, at the library, in college and maybe you just kept hanging. Sometimes it's hard to remember when the people in our lives went from being acquaintances to being friends. It used to be so simple to find a friend no matter the setting or how long you happened to know them. You would just march up to someone who looked nice and ask them to play. The funny thing is, that's really all there is to it when you're an adult, too. Is asking someone out to coffee really all that different from asking someone to play with you?

Do you want
to be friends?
(Yes) Maybe No

Making friends as an adult is deliberate. You have to decide to make the leap from acquaintance to friend, but once you do, the steps are still the same. The more time you spend with each other, the better you'll get to know your newfound friend and the deeper your relationship will become. So, imagine yourself thirty years from now. Whom would you like to sit next to on a park bench? If you are lucky, new friends may one day be old friends.

"Each friend represents a world in us,
a world possibly not born until they
arrive, and it is only by this meeting
that a new world is born."
Anaïs Nin

DATE

My friend, please answer these questions about yourself . . .

Your name is

Your birthday is   and currently you are   years old

If you had to describe yourself in three words, they would be

When you were little, you wanted to be a

You still dream about becoming a

If you won the lottery, you would spend it on

The best book you've read so far is

One of your favorite movies is

Your favorite color is

Your favorite animal is

You love the scent of

You have a secret crush on

Your hero is

You are very good at

You want to be better at

Your one regret is

The three biggest changes in your life have been

Now, your thoughts about me . . .

If you had to describe me in three words, they would be

If I were an animal I would be a(n)

The famous person I most resemble is

If I won the lottery, I would probably spend it on

If I ruled the world, there would be

You know that I have a crush on

Two things that you appreciate most about me are

And finally, about us!

We became friends when

One of the funniest moments of our friendship was

If you and I were characters in a book, movie, or on TV, we would be

The song that reminds you of us is

The thing that we have the most in common is

Our biggest difference is

Your favorite thing about our friendship is

DATE

My friend, please answer these questions about yourself . . .

Your name is

Your birthday is   and currently you are   years old

If you had to describe yourself in three words, they would be

When you were little, you wanted to be a

You still dream about becoming a

If you won the lottery, you would spend it on

The best book you've read so far is

One of your favorite movies is

Your favorite color is

Your favorite animal is

You love the scent of

You have a secret crush on

Your hero is

You are very good at

You want to be better at

Your one regret is

The three biggest changes in your life have been

Now, your thoughts about me . . .

If you had to describe me in three words, they would be _____

_____

If I were an animal I would be a(n) _____

The famous person I most resemble is _____

If I won the lottery, I would probably spend it on _____

If I ruled the world, there would be _____

You know that I have a crush on _____

Two things that you appreciate most about me are _____

And finally, about us!

We became friends when _____

One of the funniest moments of our friendship was _____

_____

If you and I were characters in a book, movie, or on TV, we would be _____

_____

The song that reminds you of us is _____

The thing that we have the most in common is _____

Our biggest difference is _____

Your favorite thing about our friendship is _____

_____

DATE ....

My friend, please answer these questions about yourself . . .

Your name is ....

Your birthday is .... and currently you are .... years old

If you had to describe yourself in three words, they would be ....
....

When you were little, you wanted to be a ....

You still dream about becoming a ....

If you won the lottery, you would spend it on ....

The best book you've read so far is ....

One of your favorite movies is ....

Your favorite color is ....

Your favorite animal is ....

You love the scent of ....

You have a secret crush on ....

Your hero is ....

You are very good at ....

You want to be better at ....

Your one regret is ....

The three biggest changes in your life have been ....
....
....
....

Now, your thoughts about me . . .

If you had to describe me in three words, they would be

If I were an animal I would be a(n)

The famous person I most resemble is

If I won the lottery, I would probably spend it on

If I ruled the world, there would be

You know that I have a crush on

Two things that you appreciate most about me are

And finally, about us!

We became friends when

One of the funniest moments of our friendship was

If you and I were characters in a book, movie, or on TV, we would be

The song that reminds you of us is

The thing that we have the most in common is

Our biggest difference is

Your favorite thing about our friendship is

DATE ....

My friend, please answer these questions about yourself . . .

Your name is ....

Your birthday is .... and currently you are .... years old

If you had to describe yourself in three words, they would be ....

....

When you were little, you wanted to be a ....

You still dream about becoming a ....

If you won the lottery, you would spend it on ....

The best book you've read so far is ....

One of your favorite movies is ....

Your favorite color is ....

Your favorite animal is ....

You love the scent of ....

You have a secret crush on ....

Your hero is ....

You are very good at ....

You want to be better at ....

Your one regret is ....

The three biggest changes in your life have been ....

....

....

Now, your thoughts about me . . .

If you had to describe me in three words, they would be _____

_____

If I were an animal I would be a(n) _____

The famous person I most resemble is _____

If I won the lottery, I would probably spend it on _____

If I ruled the world, there would be _____

You know that I have a crush on _____

Two things that you appreciate most about me are _____

_____

And finally, about us!

We became friends when _____

One of the funniest moments of our friendship was _____

_____

If you and I were characters in a book, movie, or on TV, we would be _____

_____

The song that reminds you of us is _____

The thing that we have the most in common is _____

Our biggest difference is _____

Your favorite thing about our friendship is _____

_____

DATE ....

My friend, please answer these questions about yourself . . .

Your name is ....

Your birthday is .... and currently you are .... years old

If you had to describe yourself in three words, they would be ....

....

When you were little, you wanted to be a ....

You still dream about becoming a ....

If you won the lottery, you would spend it on ....

The best book you've read so far is ....

One of your favorite movies is ....

Your favorite color is ....

Your favorite animal is ....

You love the scent of ....

You have a secret crush on ....

Your hero is ....

You are very good at ....

You want to be better at ....

Your one regret is ....

The three biggest changes in your life have been ....

....

....

Now, your thoughts about me . . .

If you had to describe me in three words, they would be

If I were an animal I would be a(n)

The famous person I most resemble is

If I won the lottery, I would probably spend it on

If I ruled the world, there would be

You know that I have a crush on

Two things that you appreciate most about me are

And finally, about us!

We became friends when

One of the funniest moments of our friendship was

If you and I were characters in a book, movie, or on TV, we would be

The song that reminds you of us is

The thing that we have the most in common is

Our biggest difference is

Your favorite thing about our friendship is

VARIETY IS THE SPICE OF LIFE

Everyone has different priorities and a unique perspective on life, and having a good mix of friends will widen the lens of your own worldview. Do you recognize any of these types of friends in your circle?

1 THE FREE-SPIRIT inspires you to look at life differently, to trust your intuition, and to live outside the lines.

2 THE HEALTH NUT meets you at the gym, gives you advice on the latest diet trends and juice cleanses, and inspires you to take better care of yourself.

3 THE MOTIVATED ONE is reliable, structured, and driven, and encourages you to find what you're passionate about.

4 YOUR OLDEST FRIEND knows all about your past and where you came from, which often gives her a unique perspective on your present and therefore valuable insights.

"There is nothing better than a friend, unless it is a friend with chocolate."

Linda Grayson

5 **THE INDEPENDENT FRIEND** is always there for fun and new adventures. She enjoys the time she gets to herself and reminds you that you can enjoy your own alone time, too.

6 **YOUR LONG-DISTANCE FRIEND** is great for phone conversations and whirlwind weekend visits; it always feels like you can pick up right where you left off.

7 **YOUR FRIEND AT WORK** or school understands one of the biggest parts of your day and how it impacts the other parts of your life. She's the one you go to when you need to laugh or let off steam (perhaps when the two of you should be working!).

8 **THE SOCIAL BUTTERFLY** is the one who entertains, organizes group activities, and introduces you to tons of new people.

DATE _____

My friend, please answer these questions about yourself . . .

Your name is _____

Your birthday is _____ and currently you are _____ years old

If you had to describe yourself in three words, they would be _____
_____

When you were little, you wanted to be a _____

You still dream about becoming a _____

If you won the lottery, you would spend it on _____

The best book you've read so far is _____

One of your favorite movies is _____

Your favorite color is _____

Your favorite animal is _____

You love the scent of _____

You have a secret crush on _____

Your hero is _____

You are very good at _____

You want to be better at _____

Your one regret is _____

The three biggest changes in your life have been _____
_____
_____

Now, your thoughts about me . . .

If you had to describe me in three words, they would be

If I were an animal I would be a(n)

The famous person I most resemble is

If I won the lottery, I would probably spend it on

If I ruled the world, there would be

You know that I have a crush on

Two things that you appreciate most about me are

And finally, about us!

We became friends when

One of the funniest moments of our friendship was

If you and I were characters in a book, movie, or on TV, we would be

The song that reminds you of us is

The thing that we have the most in common is

Our biggest difference is

Your favorite thing about our friendship is

DATE

My friend, please answer these questions about yourself . . .

Your name is

Your birthday is _____ and currently you are _____ years old

If you had to describe yourself in three words, they would be

When you were little, you wanted to be a

You still dream about becoming a

If you won the lottery, you would spend it on

The best book you've read so far is

One of your favorite movies is

Your favorite color is

Your favorite animal is

You love the scent of

You have a secret crush on

Your hero is

You are very good at

You want to be better at

Your one regret is

The three biggest changes in your life have been

Now, your thoughts about me . . .

If you had to describe me in three words, they would be _____

If I were an animal I would be a(n) _____

The famous person I most resemble is _____

If I won the lottery, I would probably spend it on _____

If I ruled the world, there would be _____

You know that I have a crush on _____

Two things that you appreciate most about me are _____

And finally, about us!

We became friends when _____

One of the funniest moments of our friendship was _____

If you and I were characters in a book, movie, or on TV, we would be _____

The song that reminds you of us is _____

The thing that we have the most in common is _____

Our biggest difference is _____

Your favorite thing about our friendship is _____

DATE _____

My friend, please answer these questions about yourself . . .

Your name is _____

Your birthday is _____ and currently you are _____ years old

If you had to describe yourself in three words, they would be _____

_____

When you were little, you wanted to be a _____

You still dream about becoming a _____

If you won the lottery, you would spend it on _____

The best book you've read so far is _____

One of your favorite movies is _____

Your favorite color is _____

Your favorite animal is _____

You love the scent of _____

You have a secret crush on _____

Your hero is _____

You are very good at _____

You want to be better at _____

Your one regret is _____

The three biggest changes in your life have been _____

_____

_____

_____

Now, your thoughts about me . . .

If you had to describe me in three words, they would be _____

_____

If I were an animal I would be a(n) _____

The famous person I most resemble is _____

If I won the lottery, I would probably spend it on _____

If I ruled the world, there would be _____

You know that I have a crush on _____

Two things that you appreciate most about me are _____

_____

And finally, about us!

We became friends when _____

One of the funniest moments of our friendship was _____

_____

If you and I were characters in a book, movie, or on TV, we would be _____

_____

The song that reminds you of us is _____

The thing that we have the most in common is _____

Our biggest difference is _____

Your favorite thing about our friendship is _____

_____

_____

DATE _____

My friend, please answer these questions about yourself . . .

Your name is _____

Your birthday is _____ and currently you are _____ years old

If you had to describe yourself in three words, they would be _____
_____

When you were little, you wanted to be a _____

You still dream about becoming a _____

If you won the lottery, you would spend it on _____

The best book you've read so far is _____

One of your favorite movies is _____

Your favorite color is _____

Your favorite animal is _____

You love the scent of _____

You have a secret crush on _____

Your hero is _____

You are very good at _____

You want to be better at _____

Your one regret is _____

The three biggest changes in your life have been _____
_____
_____

Now, your thoughts about me . . .

If you had to describe me in three words, they would be _____

_____

If I were an animal I would be a(n) _____

The famous person I most resemble is _____

If I won the lottery, I would probably spend it on _____

If I ruled the world, there would be _____

You know that I have a crush on _____

Two things that you appreciate most about me are _____

_____

And finally, about us!

We became friends when _____

One of the funniest moments of our friendship was _____

_____

If you and I were characters in a book, movie, or on TV, we would be _____

_____

The song that reminds you of us is _____

The thing that we have the most in common is _____

Our biggest difference is _____

Your favorite thing about our friendship is _____

_____

DATE _____

My friend, please answer these questions about yourself . . .

Your name is _____

Your birthday is _____ and currently you are _____ years old

If you had to describe yourself in three words, they would be _____

When you were little, you wanted to be a _____

You still dream about becoming a _____

If you won the lottery, you would spend it on _____

The best book you've read so far is _____

One of your favorite movies is _____

Your favorite color is _____

Your favorite animal is _____

You love the scent of _____

You have a secret crush on _____

Your hero is _____

You are very good at _____

You want to be better at _____

Your one regret is _____

The three biggest changes in your life have been _____

Now, your thoughts about me . . .

If you had to describe me in three words, they would be

If I were an animal I would be a(n)

The famous person I most resemble is

If I won the lottery, I would probably spend it on

If I ruled the world, there would be

You know that I have a crush on

Two things that you appreciate most about me are

And finally, about us!

We became friends when

One of the funniest moments of our friendship was

If you and I were characters in a book, movie, or on TV, we would be

The song that reminds you of us is

The thing that we have the most in common is

Our biggest difference is

Your favorite thing about our friendship is

Age is Just a Number

During your childhood, your friends were your classmates, neighbors, or teammates. You made friends with the people who you ended up spending the most time with, and they were all about your age and involved in many of the same activities you were. It would have been out of the ordinary to call someone more than a grade or two apart from you in school your friend.

As you get older, those delineations fade and you may find yourself having friends who don't fall into your own demographic. Age matters less and less as the years go by, and you might discover that you are kindred spirits with someone who is decades older or younger than you. You'll be drawn to one friend who is an old soul and another who is a true child at heart, and these qualities have nothing to do with that person's actual age. Every stage of life has its own challenges and advantages, and it is fun to get a mix of perspectives; to have friends to remind you of an earlier version of yourself and friends to offer insight into what is ahead.

There are also those friends that we grow up with, and while we may start out living nearly identical lives, the older we get the

"The most beautiful discovery true friends make is that they can grow separately without growing apart."
Elisabeth Foley

more our lives diverge. It can be challenging to maintain relationships under those circumstances but also rich and rewarding. It's an opportunity to grow with someone. Witnessing how a beloved friend deals with life's curveballs can help us navigate the twists and turns of our own lives. While you may end up growing into very different people, taking that journey together can connect you more deeply than any shared interest ever could.

DATE _____

My friend, please answer these questions about yourself . . .

Your name is _____

Your birthday is _____ and currently you are _____ years old

If you had to describe yourself in three words, they would be _____

_____

When you were little, you wanted to be a _____

You still dream about becoming a _____

If you won the lottery, you would spend it on _____

The best book you've read so far is _____

One of your favorite movies is _____

Your favorite color is _____

Your favorite animal is _____

You love the scent of _____

You have a secret crush on _____

Your hero is _____

You are very good at _____

You want to be better at _____

Your one regret is _____

The three biggest changes in your life have been _____

_____

_____

Now, your thoughts about me . . .

If you had to describe me in three words, they would be

If I were an animal I would be a(n)

The famous person I most resemble is

If I won the lottery, I would probably spend it on

If I ruled the world, there would be

You know that I have a crush on

Two things that you appreciate most about me are

And finally, about us!

We became friends when

One of the funniest moments of our friendship was

If you and I were characters in a book, movie, or on TV, we would be

The song that reminds you of us is

The thing that we have the most in common is

Our biggest difference is

Your favorite thing about our friendship is

DATE _____

My friend, please answer these questions about yourself . . .

Your name is _____

Your birthday is _____ and currently you are _____ years old

If you had to describe yourself in three words, they would be _____

_____

When you were little, you wanted to be a _____

You still dream about becoming a _____

If you won the lottery, you would spend it on _____

The best book you've read so far is _____

One of your favorite movies is _____

Your favorite color is _____

Your favorite animal is _____

You love the scent of _____

You have a secret crush on _____

Your hero is _____

You are very good at _____

You want to be better at _____

Your one regret is _____

The three biggest changes in your life have been _____

_____

_____

Now, your thoughts about me . . .

If you had to describe me in three words, they would be

If I were an animal I would be a(n)

The famous person I most resemble is

If I won the lottery, I would probably spend it on

If I ruled the world, there would be

You know that I have a crush on

Two things that you appreciate most about me are

And finally, about us!

We became friends when

One of the funniest moments of our friendship was

If you and I were characters in a book, movie, or on TV, we would be

The song that reminds you of us is

The thing that we have the most in common is

Our biggest difference is

Your favorite thing about our friendship is

DATE

My friend, please answer these questions about yourself . . .

Your name is

Your birthday is   and currently you are   years old

If you had to describe yourself in three words, they would be

When you were little, you wanted to be a

You still dream about becoming a

If you won the lottery, you would spend it on

The best book you've read so far is

One of your favorite movies is

Your favorite color is

Your favorite animal is

You love the scent of

You have a secret crush on

Your hero is

You are very good at

You want to be better at

Your one regret is

The three biggest changes in your life have been

Now, your thoughts about me . . .

If you had to describe me in three words, they would be

If I were an animal I would be a(n)

The famous person I most resemble is

If I won the lottery, I would probably spend it on

If I ruled the world, there would be

You know that I have a crush on

Two things that you appreciate most about me are

And finally, about us!

We became friends when

One of the funniest moments of our friendship was

If you and I were characters in a book, movie, or on TV, we would be

The song that reminds you of us is

The thing that we have the most in common is

Our biggest difference is

Your favorite thing about our friendship is

DATE

My friend, please answer these questions about yourself . . .

Your name is

Your birthday is   and currently you are   years old

If you had to describe yourself in three words, they would be

When you were little, you wanted to be a

You still dream about becoming a

If you won the lottery, you would spend it on

The best book you've read so far is

One of your favorite movies is

Your favorite color is

Your favorite animal is

You love the scent of

You have a secret crush on

Your hero is

You are very good at

You want to be better at

Your one regret is

The three biggest changes in your life have been

Now, your thoughts about me . . .

If you had to describe me in three words, they would be

If I were an animal I would be a(n)

The famous person I most resemble is

If I won the lottery, I would probably spend it on

If I ruled the world, there would be

You know that I have a crush on

Two things that you appreciate most about me are

And finally, about us!

We became friends when

One of the funniest moments of our friendship was

If you and I were characters in a book, movie, or on TV, we would be

The song that reminds you of us is

The thing that we have the most in common is

Our biggest difference is

Your favorite thing about our friendship is

DATE

My friend, please answer these questions about yourself . . .

Your name is

Your birthday is _____ and currently you are _____ years old

If you had to describe yourself in three words, they would be

When you were little, you wanted to be a

You still dream about becoming a

If you won the lottery, you would spend it on

The best book you've read so far is

One of your favorite movies is

Your favorite color is

Your favorite animal is

You love the scent of

You have a secret crush on

Your hero is

You are very good at

You want to be better at

Your one regret is

The three biggest changes in your life have been

Now, your thoughts about me . . .

If you had to describe me in three words, they would be

If I were an animal I would be a(n)

The famous person I most resemble is

If I won the lottery, I would probably spend it on

If I ruled the world, there would be

You know that I have a crush on

Two things that you appreciate most about me are

And finally, about us!

We became friends when

One of the funniest moments of our friendship was

If you and I were characters in a book, movie, or on TV, we would be

The song that reminds you of us is

The thing that we have the most in common is

Our biggest difference is

Your favorite thing about our friendship is

TRY SOMETHING NEW

*Our friends are often the people who fit into our
routines, but why not try enhancing these
relationships by doing something
a little out of the ordinary?*

1 RETURN TO NATURE.
Getting outside and away from
daily distractions with your friends can
be relaxing and inspiring. Plan a spring
picnic when the trees are in bloom, go
apple picking in autumn, or take a hike
in a nearby park or nature preserve.
In these settings, conversation can be
more leisurely—definitely less intense
then catching up over coffee.

2 DO GOOD TOGETHER.
Rolling up your sleeves and
volunteering for a cause that you
care about feels even better when you
involve your friends. It builds a true
sense of community. Find out what
matters to your friends and vow to
take action together.

*"Good girls go to heaven.
Bad girls go everywhere."*
Mae West

who wants to swap
problems with me?

3 LEARN A NEW SKILL.

If you want to learn something new, taking a class with friends makes the process even more enjoyable. Something like a cooking class, woodworking, or a new hobby like painting or photography would be great to share with one friend or a group.

4 START A FRIEND TRADITION.

Lots of people celebrate "Friendsgiving" instead of traveling home on the holidays. What kind of annual tradition would you like to have with your friends? Life can get really busy, but a once-yearly gathering is often all that you need to maintain a friendship.

5 SWAP PROBLEMS.

Some friends are great at knowing and understanding how you think even better than you do, so going to them for advice on a problem could be a great help. You could each exchange notes or emails describing the problems you can't solve, and later respond with a solution.

6 ROSES AND THORNS SHARING.

The next time a group of friends gets together take turns sharing one good thing and one bad thing you each have going on in your life right now. It offers a good balance between acknowledging the difficult stuff and focusing on the positive.

DATE _____

My friend, please answer these questions about yourself . . .

Your name is _____

Your birthday is _____ and currently you are _____ years old

If you had to describe yourself in three words, they would be _____

_____

When you were little, you wanted to be a _____

You still dream about becoming a _____

If you won the lottery, you would spend it on _____

The best book you've read so far is _____

One of your favorite movies is _____

Your favorite color is _____

Your favorite animal is _____

You love the scent of _____

You have a secret crush on _____

Your hero is _____

You are very good at _____

You want to be better at _____

Your one regret is _____

The three biggest changes in your life have been _____

_____

_____

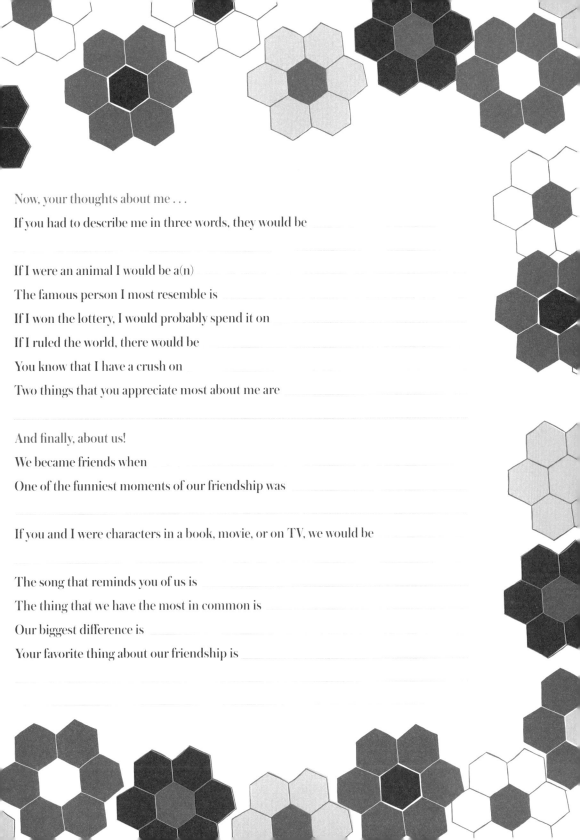

Now, your thoughts about me . . .

If you had to describe me in three words, they would be

If I were an animal I would be a(n)

The famous person I most resemble is

If I won the lottery, I would probably spend it on

If I ruled the world, there would be

You know that I have a crush on

Two things that you appreciate most about me are

And finally, about us!

We became friends when

One of the funniest moments of our friendship was

If you and I were characters in a book, movie, or on TV, we would be

The song that reminds you of us is

The thing that we have the most in common is

Our biggest difference is

Your favorite thing about our friendship is

DATE _____

My friend, please answer these questions about yourself . . .

Your name is _____

Your birthday is _____ and currently you are _____ years old

If you had to describe yourself in three words, they would be _____

_____

When you were little, you wanted to be a _____

You still dream about becoming a _____

If you won the lottery, you would spend it on _____

The best book you've read so far is _____

One of your favorite movies is _____

Your favorite color is _____

Your favorite animal is _____

You love the scent of _____

You have a secret crush on _____

Your hero is _____

You are very good at _____

You want to be better at _____

Your one regret is _____

The three biggest changes in your life have been _____

_____

_____

Now, your thoughts about me . . .

If you had to describe me in three words, they would be

If I were an animal I would be a(n)

The famous person I most resemble is

If I won the lottery, I would probably spend it on

If I ruled the world, there would be

You know that I have a crush on

Two things that you appreciate most about me are

And finally, about us!

We became friends when

One of the funniest moments of our friendship was

If you and I were characters in a book, movie, or on TV, we would be

The song that reminds you of us is

The thing that we have the most in common is

Our biggest difference is

Your favorite thing about our friendship is

DATE _____

My friend, please answer these questions about yourself . . .

Your name is _____

Your birthday is _____ and currently you are _____ years old

If you had to describe yourself in three words, they would be _____
_____

When you were little, you wanted to be a _____

You still dream about becoming a _____

If you won the lottery, you would spend it on _____

The best book you've read so far is _____

One of your favorite movies is _____

Your favorite color is _____

Your favorite animal is _____

You love the scent of _____

You have a secret crush on _____

Your hero is _____

You are very good at _____

You want to be better at _____

Your one regret is _____

The three biggest changes in your life have been _____
_____
_____

Now, your thoughts about me . . .

If you had to describe me in three words, they would be

If I were an animal I would be a(n)

The famous person I most resemble is

If I won the lottery, I would probably spend it on

If I ruled the world, there would be

You know that I have a crush on

Two things that you appreciate most about me are

And finally, about us!

We became friends when

One of the funniest moments of our friendship was

If you and I were characters in a book, movie, or on TV, we would be

The song that reminds you of us is

The thing that we have the most in common is

Our biggest difference is

Your favorite thing about our friendship is

DATE _____

My friend, please answer these questions about yourself . . .

Your name is _____

Your birthday is _____ and currently you are _____ years old

If you had to describe yourself in three words, they would be _____

_____

When you were little, you wanted to be a _____

You still dream about becoming a _____

If you won the lottery, you would spend it on _____

The best book you've read so far is _____

One of your favorite movies is _____

Your favorite color is _____

Your favorite animal is _____

You love the scent of _____

You have a secret crush on _____

Your hero is _____

You are very good at _____

You want to be better at _____

Your one regret is _____

The three biggest changes in your life have been _____

_____

_____

Now, your thoughts about me . . .

If you had to describe me in three words, they would be

If I were an animal I would be a(n)

The famous person I most resemble is

If I won the lottery, I would probably spend it on

If I ruled the world, there would be

You know that I have a crush on

Two things that you appreciate most about me are

And finally, about us!

We became friends when

One of the funniest moments of our friendship was

If you and I were characters in a book, movie, or on TV, we would be

The song that reminds you of us is

The thing that we have the most in common is

Our biggest difference is

Your favorite thing about our friendship is

DATE _____

My friend, please answer these questions about yourself . . .

Your name is _____

Your birthday is _____ and currently you are _____ years old

If you had to describe yourself in three words, they would be _____

_____

When you were little, you wanted to be a _____

You still dream about becoming a _____

If you won the lottery, you would spend it on _____

The best book you've read so far is _____

One of your favorite movies is _____

Your favorite color is _____

Your favorite animal is _____

You love the scent of _____

You have a secret crush on _____

Your hero is _____

You are very good at _____

You want to be better at _____

Your one regret is _____

The three biggest changes in your life have been _____

_____

_____

Now, your thoughts about me . . .

If you had to describe me in three words, they would be

If I were an animal I would be a(n)

The famous person I most resemble is

If I won the lottery, I would probably spend it on

If I ruled the world, there would be

You know that I have a crush on

Two things that you appreciate most about me are

And finally, about us!

We became friends when

One of the funniest moments of our friendship was

If you and I were characters in a book, movie, or on TV, we would be

The song that reminds you of us is

The thing that we have the most in common is

Our biggest difference is

Your favorite thing about our friendship is

When Worlds Collide

Mixing your friends can be extremely stressful: You may act a certain way with one friend, belong to a certain community with another, and share a particularly weird sense of humor with the third.

You have different friends for different things. One friend is the best for low-key hangs, while another friend is your first choice for going on adventures. When you have something on your mind, one of your friends listens patiently and gives great advice. Another takes you out and distracts you from your troubles with her own crazy issues. Individually, these women are all great, and one-on-one they are a perfect fit in your life.

But then your birthday comes along and you start stressing to an uncomfortable degree about the fact that you decided to invite twenty friends over, several of whom don't know each other. Or worse, they don't share the same taste. You feel responsible for making sure that everyone has a good time. What if they have nothing to talk about with the person sitting next to them? What if they have nothing in common? What if they turn out to not like each other?

If you're stressing about having all of your very different friends meet each other, think about what they do have in common: You like them and they like you. Besides, how many times have you gone to a party and been really fascinated by someone who was completely different from you? Bringing together an eclectic crowd makes things more interesting for everyone.

"Strangers are just
friends waiting
to happen."

Rob McKuen

DATE _____

My friend, please answer these questions about yourself . . .

Your name is _____

Your birthday is _____ and currently you are _____ years old

If you had to describe yourself in three words, they would be _____

_____

When you were little, you wanted to be a _____

You still dream about becoming a _____

If you won the lottery, you would spend it on _____

The best book you've read so far is _____

One of your favorite movies is _____

Your favorite color is _____

Your favorite animal is _____

You love the scent of _____

You have a secret crush on _____

Your hero is _____

You are very good at _____

You want to be better at _____

Your one regret is _____

The three biggest changes in your life have been _____

_____

_____

Now, your thoughts about me . . .

If you had to describe me in three words, they would be

If I were an animal I would be a(n)

The famous person I most resemble is

If I won the lottery, I would probably spend it on

If I ruled the world, there would be

You know that I have a crush on

Two things that you appreciate most about me are

And finally, about us!

We became friends when

One of the funniest moments of our friendship was

If you and I were characters in a book, movie, or on TV, we would be

The song that reminds you of us is

The thing that we have the most in common is

Our biggest difference is

Your favorite thing about our friendship is

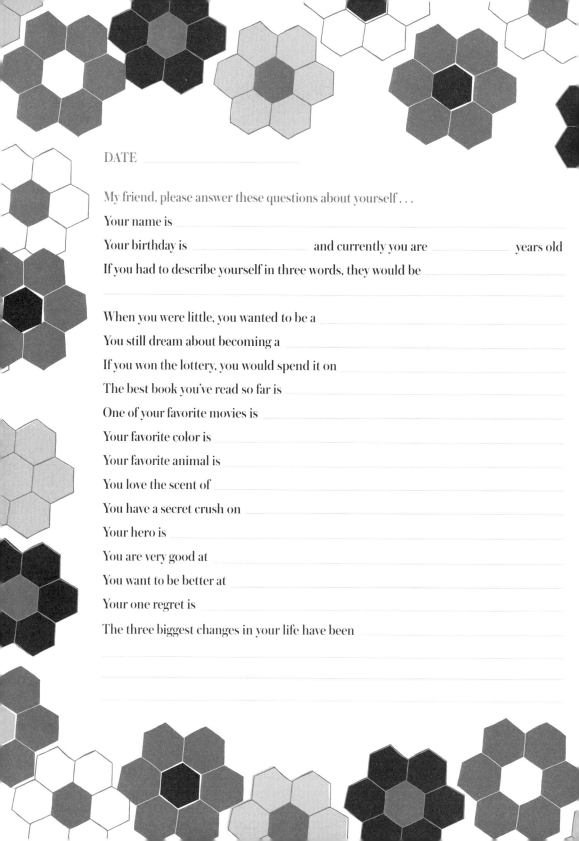

DATE _____

My friend, please answer these questions about yourself . . .

Your name is _____

Your birthday is _____ and currently you are _____ years old

If you had to describe yourself in three words, they would be _____
_____

When you were little, you wanted to be a _____

You still dream about becoming a _____

If you won the lottery, you would spend it on _____

The best book you've read so far is _____

One of your favorite movies is _____

Your favorite color is _____

Your favorite animal is _____

You love the scent of _____

You have a secret crush on _____

Your hero is _____

You are very good at _____

You want to be better at _____

Your one regret is _____

The three biggest changes in your life have been _____
_____
_____

Now, your thoughts about me . . .

If you had to describe me in three words, they would be

If I were an animal I would be a(n)

The famous person I most resemble is

If I won the lottery, I would probably spend it on

If I ruled the world, there would be

You know that I have a crush on

Two things that you appreciate most about me are

And finally, about us!

We became friends when

One of the funniest moments of our friendship was

If you and I were characters in a book, movie, or on TV, we would be

The song that reminds you of us is

The thing that we have the most in common is

Our biggest difference is

Your favorite thing about our friendship is

DATE _____

My friend, please answer these questions about yourself . . .

Your name is _____

Your birthday is _____ and currently you are _____ years old

If you had to describe yourself in three words, they would be _____
_____

When you were little, you wanted to be a _____

You still dream about becoming a _____

If you won the lottery, you would spend it on _____

The best book you've read so far is _____

One of your favorite movies is _____

Your favorite color is _____

Your favorite animal is _____

You love the scent of _____

You have a secret crush on _____

Your hero is _____

You are very good at _____

You want to be better at _____

Your one regret is _____

The three biggest changes in your life have been _____
_____
_____
_____

Now, your thoughts about me . . .

If you had to describe me in three words, they would be _____

_____

If I were an animal I would be a(n) _____

The famous person I most resemble is _____

If I won the lottery, I would probably spend it on _____

If I ruled the world, there would be _____

You know that I have a crush on _____

Two things that you appreciate most about me are _____

_____

And finally, about us!

We became friends when _____

One of the funniest moments of our friendship was _____

_____

If you and I were characters in a book, movie, or on TV, we would be _____

_____

The song that reminds you of us is _____

The thing that we have the most in common is _____

Our biggest difference is _____

Your favorite thing about our friendship is _____

_____

DATE _____

My friend, please answer these questions about yourself . . .

Your name is _____

Your birthday is _____ and currently you are _____ years old

If you had to describe yourself in three words, they would be _____
_____

When you were little, you wanted to be a _____

You still dream about becoming a _____

If you won the lottery, you would spend it on _____

The best book you've read so far is _____

One of your favorite movies is _____

Your favorite color is _____

Your favorite animal is _____

You love the scent of _____

You have a secret crush on _____

Your hero is _____

You are very good at _____

You want to be better at _____

Your one regret is _____

The three biggest changes in your life have been _____
_____
_____

Now, your thoughts about me . . .

If you had to describe me in three words, they would be

If I were an animal I would be a(n)

The famous person I most resemble is

If I won the lottery, I would probably spend it on

If I ruled the world, there would be

You know that I have a crush on

Two things that you appreciate most about me are

And finally, about us!

We became friends when

One of the funniest moments of our friendship was

If you and I were characters in a book, movie, or on TV, we would be

The song that reminds you of us is

The thing that we have the most in common is

Our biggest difference is

Your favorite thing about our friendship is

DATE

My friend, please answer these questions about yourself . . .

Your name is

Your birthday is _____ and currently you are _____ years old

If you had to describe yourself in three words, they would be

When you were little, you wanted to be a

You still dream about becoming a

If you won the lottery, you would spend it on

The best book you've read so far is

One of your favorite movies is

Your favorite color is

Your favorite animal is

You love the scent of

You have a secret crush on

Your hero is

You are very good at

You want to be better at

Your one regret is

The three biggest changes in your life have been

Now, your thoughts about me . . .

If you had to describe me in three words, they would be

If I were an animal I would be a(n)

The famous person I most resemble is

If I won the lottery, I would probably spend it on

If I ruled the world, there would be

You know that I have a crush on

Two things that you appreciate most about me are

And finally, about us!

We became friends when

One of the funniest moments of our friendship was

If you and I were characters in a book, movie, or on TV, we would be

The song that reminds you of us is

The thing that we have the most in common is

Our biggest difference is

Your favorite thing about our friendship is

"Friendship isn't a big thing, it's a million little things."
Author Unknown

WHO DOESN'T LOVE A COMPLIMENT?

The best compliments are not about a friend's appearance. Here are some ways to recognize your friends for their deeper qualities.

1 CALL OUT HER COMPETENCE.

Don't assume that your friend knows that she's especially good at something. When a friend does something that is amazing, let her know right away!

2 PRAISE HER STRENGTH.

Whether she's going through a breakup, a death in the family, an illness, or difficulties at work or at school, she'll draw confidence from your acknowledgement of her perseverance and inner strength.

3 EXPRESS GRATITUDE.
Throwing a party takes a great deal of time and energy. Offer thanks and praise to a friend who invites you into her home and makes you feel welcome. Send a hand-written note to provide her a moment to bask in the success of the gathering.

4 ACKNOWLEDGE GENEROSITY.
To the friend who is kind, thoughtful, and generous, feel free to say thank you on any random day. Maybe surprise her with flowers, for no other reason other than that you're thankful to have her in your life.

5 CELEBRATE MILESTONES.
When a friend reaches a new milestone in life, offer congratulations on her achievements. Our accomplishments mean so much more when we get to share them with friends.

6 RELISH HER PERSPECTIVE.
Let your friend know how much you appreciate her opinions, ideas, and advice. It is a wonderful thing to be praised for having the courage to live life honestly, authentically, and on one's own terms.

DATE _____

My friend, please answer these questions about yourself . . .

Your name is _____

Your birthday is _____ and currently you are _____ years old

If you had to describe yourself in three words, they would be _____
_____

When you were little, you wanted to be a _____

You still dream about becoming a _____

If you won the lottery, you would spend it on _____

The best book you've read so far is _____

One of your favorite movies is _____

Your favorite color is _____

Your favorite animal is _____

You love the scent of _____

You have a secret crush on _____

Your hero is _____

You are very good at _____

You want to be better at _____

Your one regret is _____

The three biggest changes in your life have been _____
_____
_____

Now, your thoughts about me . . .

If you had to describe me in three words, they would be _____

If I were an animal I would be a(n) _____

The famous person I most resemble is _____

If I won the lottery, I would probably spend it on _____

If I ruled the world, there would be _____

You know that I have a crush on _____

Two things that you appreciate most about me are _____

And finally, about us!

We became friends when _____

One of the funniest moments of our friendship was _____

If you and I were characters in a book, movie, or on TV, we would be _____

The song that reminds you of us is _____

The thing that we have the most in common is _____

Our biggest difference is _____

Your favorite thing about our friendship is _____

DATE _____

My friend, please answer these questions about yourself . . .

Your name is _____

Your birthday is _____ and currently you are _____ years old

If you had to describe yourself in three words, they would be _____

When you were little, you wanted to be a _____

You still dream about becoming a _____

If you won the lottery, you would spend it on _____

The best book you've read so far is _____

One of your favorite movies is _____

Your favorite color is _____

Your favorite animal is _____

You love the scent of _____

You have a secret crush on _____

Your hero is _____

You are very good at _____

You want to be better at _____

Your one regret is _____

The three biggest changes in your life have been _____

Now, your thoughts about me . . .

If you had to describe me in three words, they would be

If I were an animal I would be a(n)

The famous person I most resemble is

If I won the lottery, I would probably spend it on

If I ruled the world, there would be

You know that I have a crush on

Two things that you appreciate most about me are

And finally, about us!

We became friends when

One of the funniest moments of our friendship was

If you and I were characters in a book, movie, or on TV, we would be

The song that reminds you of us is

The thing that we have the most in common is

Our biggest difference is

Your favorite thing about our friendship is

DATE _____

My friend, please answer these questions about yourself . . .

Your name is _____

Your birthday is _____ and currently you are _____ years old

If you had to describe yourself in three words, they would be _____

_____

When you were little, you wanted to be a _____

You still dream about becoming a _____

If you won the lottery, you would spend it on _____

The best book you've read so far is _____

One of your favorite movies is _____

Your favorite color is _____

Your favorite animal is _____

You love the scent of _____

You have a secret crush on _____

Your hero is _____

You are very good at _____

You want to be better at _____

Your one regret is _____

The three biggest changes in your life have been _____

_____

_____

Now, your thoughts about me . . .

If you had to describe me in three words, they would be _____

If I were an animal I would be a(n) _____

The famous person I most resemble is _____

If I won the lottery, I would probably spend it on _____

If I ruled the world, there would be _____

You know that I have a crush on _____

Two things that you appreciate most about me are _____

And finally, about us!

We became friends when _____

One of the funniest moments of our friendship was _____

If you and I were characters in a book, movie, or on TV, we would be _____

The song that reminds you of us is _____

The thing that we have the most in common is _____

Our biggest difference is _____

Your favorite thing about our friendship is _____

DATE _____

My friend, please answer these questions about yourself . . .

Your name is _____

Your birthday is _____ and currently you are _____ years old

If you had to describe yourself in three words, they would be _____

_____

When you were little, you wanted to be a _____

You still dream about becoming a _____

If you won the lottery, you would spend it on _____

The best book you've read so far is _____

One of your favorite movies is _____

Your favorite color is _____

Your favorite animal is _____

You love the scent of _____

You have a secret crush on _____

Your hero is _____

You are very good at _____

You want to be better at _____

Your one regret is _____

The three biggest changes in your life have been _____

_____

_____

Now, your thoughts about me . . .

If you had to describe me in three words, they would be

If I were an animal I would be a(n)

The famous person I most resemble is

If I won the lottery, I would probably spend it on

If I ruled the world, there would be

You know that I have a crush on

Two things that you appreciate most about me are

And finally, about us!

We became friends when

One of the funniest moments of our friendship was

If you and I were characters in a book, movie, or on TV, we would be

The song that reminds you of us is

The thing that we have the most in common is

Our biggest difference is

Your favorite thing about our friendship is

DATE _____

My friend, please answer these questions about yourself . . .

Your name is _____

Your birthday is _____ and currently you are _____ years old

If you had to describe yourself in three words, they would be _____

_____

When you were little, you wanted to be a _____

You still dream about becoming a _____

If you won the lottery, you would spend it on _____

The best book you've read so far is _____

One of your favorite movies is _____

Your favorite color is _____

Your favorite animal is _____

You love the scent of _____

You have a secret crush on _____

Your hero is _____

You are very good at _____

You want to be better at _____

Your one regret is _____

The three biggest changes in your life have been _____

_____

_____

Now, your thoughts about me . . .

If you had to describe me in three words, they would be

If I were an animal I would be a(n)

The famous person I most resemble is

If I won the lottery, I would probably spend it on

If I ruled the world, there would be

You know that I have a crush on

Two things that you appreciate most about me are

And finally, about us!

We became friends when

One of the funniest moments of our friendship was

If you and I were characters in a book, movie, or on TV, we would be

The song that reminds you of us is

The thing that we have the most in common is

Our biggest difference is

Your favorite thing about our friendship is

Let's be Honest

Honesty is an essential part of every friendship, but how does that work in practice? Some friends may seem to think that you're some sort of confessional, spilling every detail about their lives to you, whether you feel prepared for that avalanche or not. In a way it's nice when your friends feel like they can tell you anything—but do they reciprocate? Do you find yourself always listening? Or are you the one who is always talking?

Other friends can be almost painfully honest, voicing an opinion without taking into account that you might not need or want it. You want your friends to be open and candid, but sometimes an unprompted judgment can do more harm than good. It's important to take a moment and put yourself in your friend's shoes. What are they feeling? What is their state of mind? Do they need to hear your unvarnished opinion right at this moment? Or is there a better time to discuss the issue at hand? Sometimes, all a friend needs is for you to listen and be supportive.

On the other hand, it's okay to intervene when you feel like your friend is reluctant to admit that there is a problem. Sometimes a friend needs you to step in and shake

*"Sometimes being a friend means
mastering the art of timing."*
Gloria Naylor

her out of their state of mind. The friends
who know you best, the ones who know all
of your secrets and the lies you sometimes
tell yourself, the ones you've shared your
innermost thoughts and feelings with, are the
ones who are best qualified to call you out.

Just remember to be open to what they have
to say. Friendship is all about balance. It's
about knowing when to speak up and when
to just listen.

DATE

My friend, please answer these questions about yourself . . .

Your name is

Your birthday is   and currently you are   years old

If you had to describe yourself in three words, they would be

When you were little, you wanted to be a

You still dream about becoming a

If you won the lottery, you would spend it on

The best book you've read so far is

One of your favorite movies is

Your favorite color is

Your favorite animal is

You love the scent of

You have a secret crush on

Your hero is

You are very good at

You want to be better at

Your one regret is

The three biggest changes in your life have been

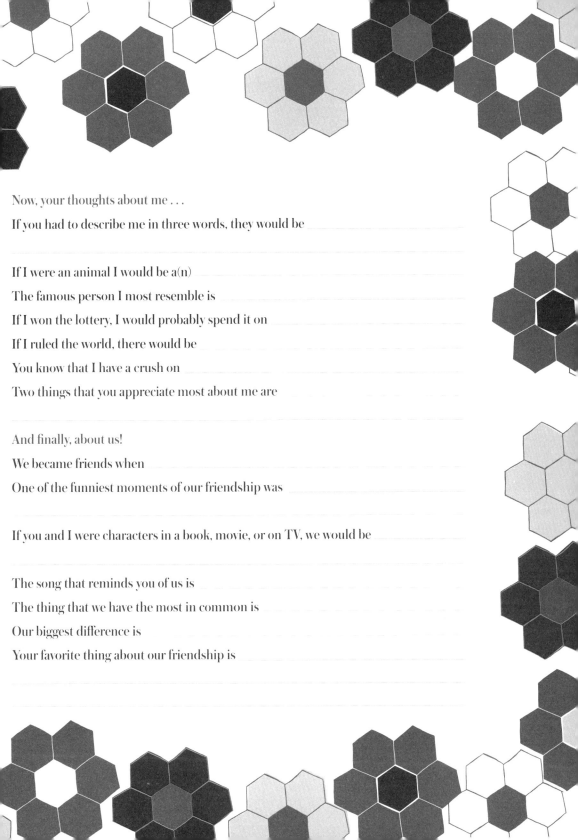

Now, your thoughts about me . . .

If you had to describe me in three words, they would be

If I were an animal I would be a(n)

The famous person I most resemble is

If I won the lottery, I would probably spend it on

If I ruled the world, there would be

You know that I have a crush on

Two things that you appreciate most about me are

And finally, about us!

We became friends when

One of the funniest moments of our friendship was

If you and I were characters in a book, movie, or on TV, we would be

The song that reminds you of us is

The thing that we have the most in common is

Our biggest difference is

Your favorite thing about our friendship is

DATE ⸺⸺⸺⸺⸺⸺⸺⸺⸺

My friend, please answer these questions about yourself . . .

Your name is ⸺⸺⸺⸺⸺⸺⸺⸺⸺⸺⸺⸺⸺

Your birthday is ⸺⸺⸺⸺⸺⸺ and currently you are ⸺⸺⸺ years old

If you had to describe yourself in three words, they would be ⸺⸺⸺⸺⸺⸺

⸺⸺⸺⸺⸺⸺⸺⸺⸺⸺⸺⸺⸺⸺⸺⸺⸺⸺⸺

When you were little, you wanted to be a ⸺⸺⸺⸺⸺⸺⸺⸺⸺

You still dream about becoming a ⸺⸺⸺⸺⸺⸺⸺⸺⸺⸺⸺

If you won the lottery, you would spend it on ⸺⸺⸺⸺⸺⸺⸺⸺

The best book you've read so far is ⸺⸺⸺⸺⸺⸺⸺⸺⸺⸺

One of your favorite movies is ⸺⸺⸺⸺⸺⸺⸺⸺⸺⸺⸺

Your favorite color is ⸺⸺⸺⸺⸺⸺⸺⸺⸺⸺⸺⸺⸺

Your favorite animal is ⸺⸺⸺⸺⸺⸺⸺⸺⸺⸺⸺⸺⸺

You love the scent of ⸺⸺⸺⸺⸺⸺⸺⸺⸺⸺⸺⸺⸺

You have a secret crush on ⸺⸺⸺⸺⸺⸺⸺⸺⸺⸺⸺⸺

Your hero is ⸺⸺⸺⸺⸺⸺⸺⸺⸺⸺⸺⸺⸺⸺⸺⸺

You are very good at ⸺⸺⸺⸺⸺⸺⸺⸺⸺⸺⸺⸺⸺

You want to be better at ⸺⸺⸺⸺⸺⸺⸺⸺⸺⸺⸺⸺

Your one regret is ⸺⸺⸺⸺⸺⸺⸺⸺⸺⸺⸺⸺⸺⸺

The three biggest changes in your life have been ⸺⸺⸺⸺⸺⸺⸺

⸺⸺⸺⸺⸺⸺⸺⸺⸺⸺⸺⸺⸺⸺⸺⸺⸺⸺⸺

⸺⸺⸺⸺⸺⸺⸺⸺⸺⸺⸺⸺⸺⸺⸺⸺⸺⸺⸺

Now, your thoughts about me . . .

If you had to describe me in three words, they would be _____

If I were an animal I would be a(n) _____

The famous person I most resemble is _____

If I won the lottery, I would probably spend it on _____

If I ruled the world, there would be _____

You know that I have a crush on _____

Two things that you appreciate most about me are _____

And finally, about us!

We became friends when _____

One of the funniest moments of our friendship was _____

If you and I were characters in a book, movie, or on TV, we would be _____

The song that reminds you of us is _____

The thing that we have the most in common is _____

Our biggest difference is _____

Your favorite thing about our friendship is _____

DATE _____

My friend, please answer these questions about yourself . . .

Your name is _____

Your birthday is _____ and currently you are _____ years old

If you had to describe yourself in three words, they would be
_____

When you were little, you wanted to be a _____

You still dream about becoming a _____

If you won the lottery, you would spend it on _____

The best book you've read so far is _____

One of your favorite movies is _____

Your favorite color is _____

Your favorite animal is _____

You love the scent of _____

You have a secret crush on _____

Your hero is _____

You are very good at _____

You want to be better at _____

Your one regret is _____

The three biggest changes in your life have been
_____
_____

Now, your thoughts about me . . .

If you had to describe me in three words, they would be

If I were an animal I would be a(n)

The famous person I most resemble is

If I won the lottery, I would probably spend it on

If I ruled the world, there would be

You know that I have a crush on

Two things that you appreciate most about me are

And finally, about us!

We became friends when

One of the funniest moments of our friendship was

If you and I were characters in a book, movie, or on TV, we would be

The song that reminds you of us is

The thing that we have the most in common is

Our biggest difference is

Your favorite thing about our friendship is

DATE _____ _____

My friend, please answer these questions about yourself . . .

Your name is _____

Your birthday is _____ and currently you are _____ years old

If you had to describe yourself in three words, they would be _____

_____

When you were little, you wanted to be a _____

You still dream about becoming a _____

If you won the lottery, you would spend it on _____

The best book you've read so far is _____

One of your favorite movies is _____

Your favorite color is _____

Your favorite animal is _____

You love the scent of _____

You have a secret crush on _____

Your hero is _____

You are very good at _____

You want to be better at _____

Your one regret is _____

The three biggest changes in your life have been _____

_____

_____

Now, your thoughts about me . . .

If you had to describe me in three words, they would be _____

If I were an animal I would be a(n) _____

The famous person I most resemble is _____

If I won the lottery, I would probably spend it on _____

If I ruled the world, there would be _____

You know that I have a crush on _____

Two things that you appreciate most about me are _____

And finally, about us!

We became friends when _____

One of the funniest moments of our friendship was _____

If you and I were characters in a book, movie, or on TV, we would be _____

The song that reminds you of us is _____

The thing that we have the most in common is _____

Our biggest difference is _____

Your favorite thing about our friendship is _____

DATE _____

My friend, please answer these questions about yourself . . .

Your name is _____

Your birthday is _____ and currently you are _____ years old

If you had to describe yourself in three words, they would be _____

_____

When you were little, you wanted to be a _____

You still dream about becoming a _____

If you won the lottery, you would spend it on _____

The best book you've read so far is _____

One of your favorite movies is _____

Your favorite color is _____

Your favorite animal is _____

You love the scent of _____

You have a secret crush on _____

Your hero is _____

You are very good at _____

You want to be better at _____

Your one regret is _____

The three biggest changes in your life have been _____

_____

_____

Now, your thoughts about me . . .

If you had to describe me in three words, they would be

If I were an animal I would be a(n)

The famous person I most resemble is

If I won the lottery, I would probably spend it on

If I ruled the world, there would be

You know that I have a crush on

Two things that you appreciate most about me are

And finally, about us!

We became friends when

One of the funniest moments of our friendship was

If you and I were characters in a book, movie, or on TV, we would be

The song that reminds you of us is

The thing that we have the most in common is

Our biggest difference is

Your favorite thing about our friendship is

A FRIEND FOR EVERY NEED

Just as you have friends with various priorities and goals, it's important to have friends who play different emotional roles in your life. Which ones are most significant to you?

Want to go for a walk?

1 THE ONE WHO BEARS WITNESS. It's important to have someone who is there when things go well and when they don't. This friend knows your past challenges and is therefore able to testify how far you've come.

2 THE ONE WHO TALKS FOR HOURS. Are you someone who likes to discuss emotional issues that don't really have answers? Then you need a friend who doesn't need a conversation to come to a conclusion. Sharing with one another is half the point.

3 THE ONE WHO WILL INDULGE. Everyone needs a little relief from discipline now and again. It's great to have someone who takes the view that ruining your diet with a friend is not actually ruining a diet; it's enjoying a piece of cake in good company.

what do you think i should do?

4 THE ONE WHO DOESN'T
JUDGE. Did you do something
embarrassing? As soon as you have
told it to a good friend, it is not
embarrassing anymore. It is a good
story!

5 THE ONE WHO EMPATHIZES.
Having someone play devil's ad-
vocate isn't always welcome. Sometimes you just want to turn to the
person who instantly understands
your dilemmas and commiserates
with your point of view.

6 THE ONE WHO QUESTIONS.
An honest friend will let you know
if she disagrees with you. Depending
on the situation this can be tough, but
there are times when you need someone to hold up a mirror and ask
if you're happy with what you see.

*"The best time to make friends
is before you need them."*
Ethel Barrymore

DATE

My friend, please answer these questions about yourself . . .

Your name is

Your birthday is _____ and currently you are _____ years old

If you had to describe yourself in three words, they would be

When you were little, you wanted to be a

You still dream about becoming a

If you won the lottery, you would spend it on

The best book you've read so far is

One of your favorite movies is

Your favorite color is

Your favorite animal is

You love the scent of

You have a secret crush on

Your hero is

You are very good at

You want to be better at

Your one regret is

The three biggest changes in your life have been

Now, your thoughts about me . . .

If you had to describe me in three words, they would be _____

If I were an animal I would be a(n) _____

The famous person I most resemble is _____

If I won the lottery, I would probably spend it on _____

If I ruled the world, there would be _____

You know that I have a crush on _____

Two things that you appreciate most about me are _____

And finally, about us!

We became friends when _____

One of the funniest moments of our friendship was _____

If you and I were characters in a book, movie, or on TV, we would be _____

The song that reminds you of us is _____

The thing that we have the most in common is _____

Our biggest difference is _____

Your favorite thing about our friendship is _____

DATE _____

My friend, please answer these questions about yourself . . .

Your name is _____

Your birthday is _____ and currently you are _____ years old

If you had to describe yourself in three words, they would be _____

_____

When you were little, you wanted to be a _____

You still dream about becoming a _____

If you won the lottery, you would spend it on _____

The best book you've read so far is _____

One of your favorite movies is _____

Your favorite color is _____

Your favorite animal is _____

You love the scent of _____

You have a secret crush on _____

Your hero is _____

You are very good at _____

You want to be better at _____

Your one regret is _____

The three biggest changes in your life have been _____

_____

Now, your thoughts about me . . .

If you had to describe me in three words, they would be

If I were an animal I would be a(n)

The famous person I most resemble is

If I won the lottery, I would probably spend it on

If I ruled the world, there would be

You know that I have a crush on

Two things that you appreciate most about me are

And finally, about us!

We became friends when

One of the funniest moments of our friendship was

If you and I were characters in a book, movie, or on TV, we would be

The song that reminds you of us is

The thing that we have the most in common is

Our biggest difference is

Your favorite thing about our friendship is

DATE ....

My friend, please answer these questions about yourself . . .

Your name is ....

Your birthday is .... and currently you are .... years old

If you had to describe yourself in three words, they would be ....
....

When you were little, you wanted to be a ....

You still dream about becoming a ....

If you won the lottery, you would spend it on ....

The best book you've read so far is ....

One of your favorite movies is ....

Your favorite color is ....

Your favorite animal is ....

You love the scent of ....

You have a secret crush on ....

Your hero is ....

You are very good at ....

You want to be better at ....

Your one regret is ....

The three biggest changes in your life have been ....
....
....

Now, your thoughts about me . . .

If you had to describe me in three words, they would be

_____

If I were an animal I would be a(n) _____

The famous person I most resemble is _____

If I won the lottery, I would probably spend it on _____

If I ruled the world, there would be _____

You know that I have a crush on _____

Two things that you appreciate most about me are _____

And finally, about us!

We became friends when _____

One of the funniest moments of our friendship was _____

_____

If you and I were characters in a book, movie, or on TV, we would be _____

_____

The song that reminds you of us is _____

The thing that we have the most in common is _____

Our biggest difference is _____

Your favorite thing about our friendship is _____

_____

DATE _____

My friend, please answer these questions about yourself . . .

Your name is _____

Your birthday is _____ and currently you are _____ years old

If you had to describe yourself in three words, they would be _____
_____

When you were little, you wanted to be a _____

You still dream about becoming a _____

If you won the lottery, you would spend it on _____

The best book you've read so far is _____

One of your favorite movies is _____

Your favorite color is _____

Your favorite animal is _____

You love the scent of _____

You have a secret crush on _____

Your hero is _____

You are very good at _____

You want to be better at _____

Your one regret is _____

The three biggest changes in your life have been _____
_____
_____

Now, your thoughts about me . . .

If you had to describe me in three words, they would be

If I were an animal I would be a(n)

The famous person I most resemble is

If I won the lottery, I would probably spend it on

If I ruled the world, there would be

You know that I have a crush on

Two things that you appreciate most about me are

And finally, about us!

We became friends when

One of the funniest moments of our friendship was

If you and I were characters in a book, movie, or on TV, we would be

The song that reminds you of us is

The thing that we have the most in common is

Our biggest difference is

Your favorite thing about our friendship is

DATE _____

My friend, please answer these questions about yourself . . .

Your name is _____

Your birthday is _____ and currently you are _____ years old

If you had to describe yourself in three words, they would be _____

_____

When you were little, you wanted to be a _____

You still dream about becoming a _____

If you won the lottery, you would spend it on _____

The best book you've read so far is _____

One of your favorite movies is _____

Your favorite color is _____

Your favorite animal is _____

You love the scent of _____

You have a secret crush on _____

Your hero is _____

You are very good at _____

You want to be better at _____

Your one regret is _____

The three biggest changes in your life have been _____

_____

_____

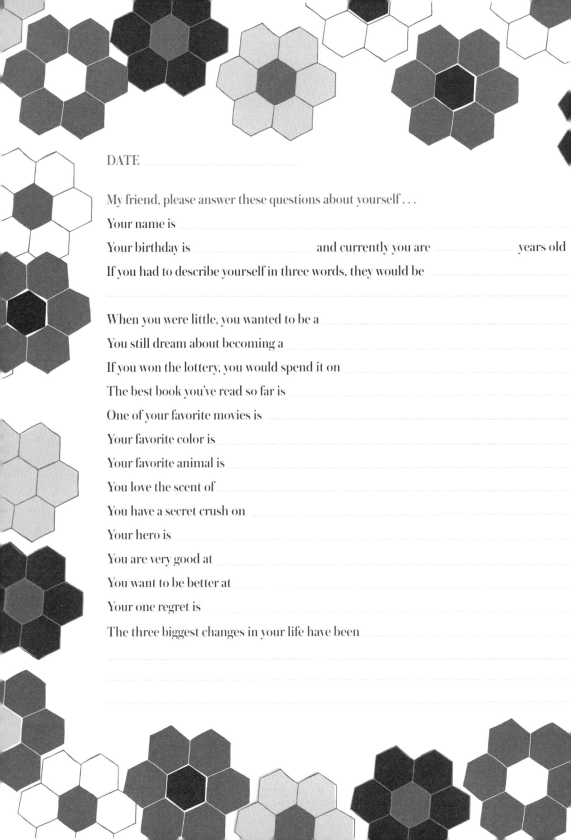

Now, your thoughts about me . . .

If you had to describe me in three words, they would be

If I were an animal I would be a(n)

The famous person I most resemble is

If I won the lottery, I would probably spend it on

If I ruled the world, there would be

You know that I have a crush on

Two things that you appreciate most about me are

And finally, about us!

We became friends when

One of the funniest moments of our friendship was

If you and I were characters in a book, movie, or on TV, we would be

The song that reminds you of us is

The thing that we have the most in common is

Our biggest difference is

Your favorite thing about our friendship is

When There Are No Words

Funerals can be heartbreaking. When you attend one, you have to face the terrifying prospect of seeing so many grieving people, and it can feel like such an invasion of privacy to see someone you know with her guard down so completely, perhaps struggling to appear strong, secure, and keeping it together.

When you're at a funeral, it's important to recognize that you're probably not just crying for the people at the service or for the person who has passed away, but also for things in your own life. Tragedy can have a way of putting things in perspective. As the years pass by, you and your friends will see more of each other's pain: deaths, heartbreak, people sending their parents to nursing homes. This is where you'll be put to the test, more than you may realize right now. Maybe you're worried you'll say the wrong thing. "My condolences," sounds too stiff. "I'm so sorry," feels like it's not enough. Maybe you don't have the right words, maybe you're afraid that heartbreak is contagious, but if you don't turn up when your friend needs you the most, she might find that she no longer needs you at all.

Even if you can't find the words, sometimes all your friend needs is a hug to let her know she's not alone. Remind her that though a person may be gone, they still live on in all the little moments you remember. Take some time and celebrate those happy memories together.

"I would rather walk with a friend in the dark, than alone in the light."
Helen Keller

DATE _____

My friend, please answer these questions about yourself . . .

Your name is _____

Your birthday is _____ and currently you are _____ years old

If you had to describe yourself in three words, they would be _____

When you were little, you wanted to be a _____

You still dream about becoming a _____

If you won the lottery, you would spend it on _____

The best book you've read so far is _____

One of your favorite movies is _____

Your favorite color is _____

Your favorite animal is _____

You love the scent of _____

You have a secret crush on _____

Your hero is _____

You are very good at _____

You want to be better at _____

Your one regret is _____

The three biggest changes in your life have been _____

Now, your thoughts about me . . .

If you had to describe me in three words, they would be

If I were an animal I would be a(n)

The famous person I most resemble is

If I won the lottery, I would probably spend it on

If I ruled the world, there would be

You know that I have a crush on

Two things that you appreciate most about me are

And finally, about us!

We became friends when

One of the funniest moments of our friendship was

If you and I were characters in a book, movie, or on TV, we would be

The song that reminds you of us is

The thing that we have the most in common is

Our biggest difference is

Your favorite thing about our friendship is

DATE

My friend, please answer these questions about yourself . . .

Your name is

Your birthday is   and currently you are   years old

If you had to describe yourself in three words, they would be

When you were little, you wanted to be a

You still dream about becoming a

If you won the lottery, you would spend it on

The best book you've read so far is

One of your favorite movies is

Your favorite color is

Your favorite animal is

You love the scent of

You have a secret crush on

Your hero is

You are very good at

You want to be better at

Your one regret is

The three biggest changes in your life have been

Now, your thoughts about me . . .

If you had to describe me in three words, they would be

If I were an animal I would be a(n)

The famous person I most resemble is

If I won the lottery, I would probably spend it on

If I ruled the world, there would be

You know that I have a crush on

Two things that you appreciate most about me are

And finally, about us!

We became friends when

One of the funniest moments of our friendship was

If you and I were characters in a book, movie, or on TV, we would be

The song that reminds you of us is

The thing that we have the most in common is

Our biggest difference is

Your favorite thing about our friendship is

DATE

My friend, please answer these questions about yourself . . .

Your name is

Your birthday is _____ and currently you are _____ years old

If you had to describe yourself in three words, they would be

When you were little, you wanted to be a

You still dream about becoming a

If you won the lottery, you would spend it on

The best book you've read so far is

One of your favorite movies is

Your favorite color is

Your favorite animal is

You love the scent of

You have a secret crush on

Your hero is

You are very good at

You want to be better at

Your one regret is

The three biggest changes in your life have been

Now, your thoughts about me . . .

If you had to describe me in three words, they would be

If I were an animal I would be a(n)

The famous person I most resemble is

If I won the lottery, I would probably spend it on

If I ruled the world, there would be

You know that I have a crush on

Two things that you appreciate most about me are

And finally, about us!

We became friends when

One of the funniest moments of our friendship was

If you and I were characters in a book, movie, or on TV, we would be

The song that reminds you of us is

The thing that we have the most in common is

Our biggest difference is

Your favorite thing about our friendship is

DATE

My friend, please answer these questions about yourself . . .

Your name is

Your birthday is _____ and currently you are _____ years old

If you had to describe yourself in three words, they would be

When you were little, you wanted to be a

You still dream about becoming a

If you won the lottery, you would spend it on

The best book you've read so far is

One of your favorite movies is

Your favorite color is

Your favorite animal is

You love the scent of

You have a secret crush on

Your hero is

You are very good at

You want to be better at

Your one regret is

The three biggest changes in your life have been

Now, your thoughts about me . . .

If you had to describe me in three words, they would be

If I were an animal I would be a(n)

The famous person I most resemble is

If I won the lottery, I would probably spend it on

If I ruled the world, there would be

You know that I have a crush on

Two things that you appreciate most about me are

And finally, about us!

We became friends when

One of the funniest moments of our friendship was

If you and I were characters in a book, movie, or on TV, we would be

The song that reminds you of us is

The thing that we have the most in common is

Our biggest difference is

Your favorite thing about our friendship is

DATE

My friend, please answer these questions about yourself . . .

Your name is

Your birthday is   and currently you are   years old

If you had to describe yourself in three words, they would be

When you were little, you wanted to be a

You still dream about becoming a

If you won the lottery, you would spend it on

The best book you've read so far is

One of your favorite movies is

Your favorite color is

Your favorite animal is

You love the scent of

You have a secret crush on

Your hero is

You are very good at

You want to be better at

Your one regret is

The three biggest changes in your life have been

Now, your thoughts about me . . .

If you had to describe me in three words, they would be

If I were an animal I would be a(n)

The famous person I most resemble is

If I won the lottery, I would probably spend it on

If I ruled the world, there would be

You know that I have a crush on

Two things that you appreciate most about me are

And finally, about us!

We became friends when

One of the funniest moments of our friendship was

If you and I were characters in a book, movie, or on TV, we would be

The song that reminds you of us is

The thing that we have the most in common is

Our biggest difference is

Your favorite thing about our friendship is

NOBODY IS PERFECT

No one enjoys the feeling of jealousy, particularly when you are envious of your friends. When you feel jealous of a friend, it usually has less to do with the fact that she is perfect (she isn't) and more to do with the challenges you are facing in your own life. Try to forgive yourself and look to your friends for inspiration.

1 BODY ENVY. It's easy to be jealous of a friend who has recently lost weight or is in great shape. Instead, look for encouragement in her health successes. Follow her example by making more mindful choices about your own health. Ask her to be your gym buddy so you can help each other maintain a healthy lifestyle.

2 STYLE ENVY. Some people seem to have everything together and always look great or have the latest fashion trend mastered. Take this as a chance to revamp your own fashion sense and ask your friend to take you shopping, or arrange a clothing swap among a group of friends for a fun-filled activity that will refresh your wardrobe without the expense.

3 NEW FRIEND ENVY. Maybe a friend of yours has started hanging out with new people, and you just don't move in their circles. Remember that new friends don't replace the old ones. There is room in life for more than one friend. If you feel a little neglected by someone you are close to, arrange a special date for just the two of you to catch up.

4 SUCCESS ENVY. It can be difficult to watch a friend gather accolades or rise in her career, particularly if you're feeling stuck or frustrated. Again, follow her example by making more strategic choices about your own pursuits. Take her out to coffee and get the inside scoop on what moves she made to put her star on the rise.

5 RELATIONSHIP ENVY. It's easy to feel jealous when hearing a friend talk about her partner and the wonderful things they do or say. If you are in a relationship, follow your friend's example and focus on the unique things that you appreciate in your partner. Your relationship may not be exactly like hers, and that's OK. If you are single, make note of the things that you're looking for in a partnership.

"Anybody can sympathize with the sufferings of a friend, but it requires a very fine nature to sympathize with a friend's success."
Oscar Wilde

6 CONTROL ENVY. When you're struggling with a problem or dealing with a hard time, it's easy to feel jealous of the friend who seems to have everything in order. Keep in mind that everyone has their challenges, whether or not they are immediately visible. If it seems like your friend is excelling at a particular aspect of her life, ask her how she does it.

DATE ....

My friend, please answer these questions about yourself . . .

Your name is ....

Your birthday is .... and currently you are .... years old

If you had to describe yourself in three words, they would be ....

....

When you were little, you wanted to be a ....

You still dream about becoming a ....

If you won the lottery, you would spend it on ....

The best book you've read so far is ....

One of your favorite movies is ....

Your favorite color is ....

Your favorite animal is ....

You love the scent of ....

You have a secret crush on ....

Your hero is ....

You are very good at ....

You want to be better at ....

Your one regret is ....

The three biggest changes in your life have been ....

....

....

Now, your thoughts about me . . .

If you had to describe me in three words, they would be

If I were an animal I would be a(n)

The famous person I most resemble is

If I won the lottery, I would probably spend it on

If I ruled the world, there would be

You know that I have a crush on

Two things that you appreciate most about me are

And finally, about us!

We became friends when

One of the funniest moments of our friendship was

If you and I were characters in a book, movie, or on TV, we would be

The song that reminds you of us is

The thing that we have the most in common is

Our biggest difference is

Your favorite thing about our friendship is

DATE _____

My friend, please answer these questions about yourself . . .

Your name is _____

Your birthday is _____ and currently you are _____ years old

If you had to describe yourself in three words, they would be _____
_____

When you were little, you wanted to be a _____

You still dream about becoming a _____

If you won the lottery, you would spend it on _____

The best book you've read so far is _____

One of your favorite movies is _____

Your favorite color is _____

Your favorite animal is _____

You love the scent of _____

You have a secret crush on _____

Your hero is _____

You are very good at _____

You want to be better at _____

Your one regret is _____

The three biggest changes in your life have been _____
_____
_____

Now, your thoughts about me . . .

If you had to describe me in three words, they would be _____

_____

If I were an animal I would be a(n) _____

The famous person I most resemble is _____

If I won the lottery, I would probably spend it on _____

If I ruled the world, there would be _____

You know that I have a crush on _____

Two things that you appreciate most about me are _____

_____

And finally, about us!

We became friends when _____

One of the funniest moments of our friendship was _____

_____

If you and I were characters in a book, movie, or on TV, we would be _____

_____

The song that reminds you of us is _____

The thing that we have the most in common is _____

Our biggest difference is _____

Your favorite thing about our friendship is _____

_____

DATE

My friend, please answer these questions about yourself . . .

Your name is

Your birthday is   and currently you are   years old

If you had to describe yourself in three words, they would be

When you were little, you wanted to be a

You still dream about becoming a

If you won the lottery, you would spend it on

The best book you've read so far is

One of your favorite movies is

Your favorite color is

Your favorite animal is

You love the scent of

You have a secret crush on

Your hero is

You are very good at

You want to be better at

Your one regret is

The three biggest changes in your life have been

Now, your thoughts about me . . .

If you had to describe me in three words, they would be

If I were an animal I would be a(n)

The famous person I most resemble is

If I won the lottery, I would probably spend it on

If I ruled the world, there would be

You know that I have a crush on

Two things that you appreciate most about me are

And finally, about us!

We became friends when

One of the funniest moments of our friendship was

If you and I were characters in a book, movie, or on TV, we would be

The song that reminds you of us is

The thing that we have the most in common is

Our biggest difference is

Your favorite thing about our friendship is

DATE

My friend, please answer these questions about yourself . . .

Your name is

Your birthday is _____ and currently you are _____ years old

If you had to describe yourself in three words, they would be

When you were little, you wanted to be a

You still dream about becoming a

If you won the lottery, you would spend it on

The best book you've read so far is

One of your favorite movies is

Your favorite color is

Your favorite animal is

You love the scent of

You have a secret crush on

Your hero is

You are very good at

You want to be better at

Your one regret is

The three biggest changes in your life have been

Now, your thoughts about me . . .

If you had to describe me in three words, they would be

If I were an animal I would be a(n)

The famous person I most resemble is

If I won the lottery, I would probably spend it on

If I ruled the world, there would be

You know that I have a crush on

Two things that you appreciate most about me are

And finally, about us!

We became friends when

One of the funniest moments of our friendship was

If you and I were characters in a book, movie, or on TV, we would be

The song that reminds you of us is

The thing that we have the most in common is

Our biggest difference is

Your favorite thing about our friendship is

DATE _____

My friend, please answer these questions about yourself . . .

Your name is _____

Your birthday is _____ and currently you are _____ years old

If you had to describe yourself in three words, they would be _____
_____

When you were little, you wanted to be a _____

You still dream about becoming a _____

If you won the lottery, you would spend it on _____

The best book you've read so far is _____

One of your favorite movies is _____

Your favorite color is _____

Your favorite animal is _____

You love the scent of _____

You have a secret crush on _____

Your hero is _____

You are very good at _____

You want to be better at _____

Your one regret is _____

The three biggest changes in your life have been _____
_____
_____
_____

Now, your thoughts about me . . .

If you had to describe me in three words, they would be _____

_____

If I were an animal I would be a(n) _____

The famous person I most resemble is _____

If I won the lottery, I would probably spend it on _____

If I ruled the world, there would be _____

You know that I have a crush on _____

Two things that you appreciate most about me are _____

_____

And finally, about us!

We became friends when _____

One of the funniest moments of our friendship was _____

_____

If you and I were characters in a book, movie, or on TV, we would be _____

_____

The song that reminds you of us is _____

The thing that we have the most in common is _____

Our biggest difference is _____

Your favorite thing about our friendship is _____

Friends Forever?

People grow and change as they go through their lives and friendships grow and change with them. Sometimes people grow apart naturally. Your drift in different directions, other people enter your lives, and you lose touch.

But what if the friendship becomes confining or draining or otherwise unhealthy? Friendships are just as complex as romantic relationships, and there's nothing unusual about breaking up with someone you've been dating if the relationship isn't working. So why should friendship be any different?

Deliberately breaking up with a friend can be incredibly difficult. Sometimes the friend you needed at a certain point in your life isn't necessarily someone who can be a good friend to you later in life. Coming to that understanding can be a very painful process. Maybe they have grown into someone you struggle to be close to. Or perhaps you've grown into someone new and they still try to squeeze you back into the person you used to be. You may feel that they are holding you back in some way. Or maybe you keep pouring all your energy into making the friendship work and they aren't reciprocating. In all of these instances, it's

Dear Friend

"I have lost friends, some by death . . .
others through sheer inability to cross the street."
Virginia Woolf

important to know when to move on and to understand that it is acceptable to do so. Not all the friendships you have will be life long and that's OK.

Cherish who that friend was to you, appreciate the memories you have of them and the good things that came from your relationship, and then let them go.

THE FRIENDSHIP BOOK
Design by Lisa Grue and Sabine Brandt

Illustrations by Lisa Grue

ISBN 978-1-4197-2693-4

© 2015 Lisa Grue and Maise Njor

Originally published in Danish by Lindhardt og Ringhof Forlag

English translation © 2018 Abrams Noterie

Printed and bound in China

10 9 8 7 6 5 4 3 2 1

Abrams Noterie products are available at special discounts when
purchased in quantity for premiums and promotions as well as
fundraising or educational use.

ABRAMS The Art of Books
195 Broadway, New York, NY 10007
abramsbooks.com